Archaeology

Cool Women Who Dig

Anita Yasuda

Illustrated by
Lena Chandhok

Nomad Press
A division of Nomad Communications
10 9 8 7 6 5 4 3 2 1

This book was manufactured by CGB Printers,
North Mankato, Minnesota, United States
April 2017, Job #220016

ISBN Softcover: 978-1-61930-500-7
ISBN Hardcover: 978-1-61930-496-3

Educational Consultant, Marla Conn

Questions regarding the ordering of this book should be addressed to
Nomad Press
2456 Christian St.
White River Junction, VT 05001
www.nomadpress.net

Printed in the United States.

~ Other titles in the Girls in Science Series ~

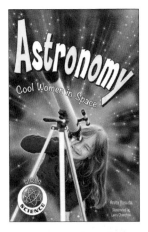

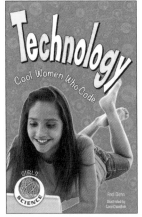

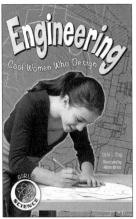

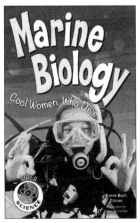

Check out more titles at www.nomadpress.net

How to Use This Book

In this book you'll find a few different ways to explore the topic of women in archaeology.

The essential questions in each Ask & Answer box encourage you to think further. You probably won't find the answers to these questions in the text, and sometimes there are no right or wrong answers! Instead, these questions are here to help you think more deeply about what you're reading and how the material connects to your own life.

There's a lot of new vocabulary in this book! Can you figure out a word's meaning from the paragraph? Look in the glossary in the back of the book to find the definitions of words you don't know.

Are you interested in what women have to say about archaeology? You'll find quotes from women who are professionals in the archaeology field. You can learn a lot by listening to people who have worked hard to succeed!

Primary sources come from people who were eyewitnesses to events. They might write about the event, take pictures, or record the event for radio or video. Why are primary sources important?

Interested in primary sources? Look for this icon.

Use a QR code reader app on your tablet or other device to find online primary sources. You can find a list of URLs on the Resources page. If the QR code doesn't work, try searching the Internet with the Keyword Prompts to find other helpful sources.

CONTENTS

INTRODUCTION
The Study of Long Ago

Have you ever wondered what life was like
long ago? Archaeologists do. They are curious
about the past and how it can influence the
future. Their work takes place in offices, labs,
national parks, museums, and on sites all over
the world. They might uncover petroglyphs
carved onto the walls of remote canyons
or ancient ruins buried beneath a modern
office building. Archaeologists investigate
industrial sites, such as gold mines, dive to
historic shipwrecks, or scale mountaintops.

Some archaeologists preserve these sites and artifacts with illustrations. They might work in labs using various tools to examine, date, and analyze archaeological materials, such as shells and bones, clothing, and tools. Archaeologists can work with communities to explore history together.

In the past few years, archaeologists have made many amazing discoveries. These include 400-year-old graves at the Jamestown settlement in Virginia and a lost city in Central America. They've found an eighteenth-century Spanish galleon loaded with treasure and a possible secret chamber in an Egyptian pharaoh's tomb.

Archaeologists sometimes use cutting-edge tools. Space archaeologist Sarah Parcak and her team might have discovered a new Viking site in North America. Sarah uses satellite images to find threats to archaeological sites and to locate new sites to investigate.

A professor at the University of Alabama at Birmingham, she spends many hours researching images. Her work has led to the discovery of thousands of ancient Egyptian sites, including lost pyramids.

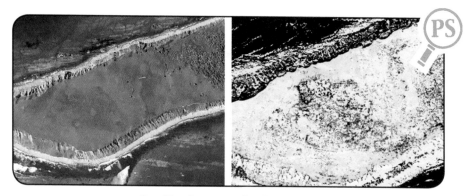

Satellite images of Point Rosee
photo credit: © 2016 DigitalGlobe

In 2015, Sarah and her international team of researchers were investigating a site of interest at Point Rosee. This is on the southwestern coast of Newfoundland, Canada.

Using trowels and brushes, they peeled away layers of grass and found a big surprise. The team discovered a hearth that had been used for cooking bog iron. They also found turf walls similar to those built by the Vikings.

More research is needed to definitely determine that this is a Viking site. If these astonishing discoveries are confirmed, this will be only the second Viking settlement ever found in North America. Who knows what else Sarah and her team will discover!

WHAT IS ARCHAEOLOGY?

In many popular movies, archaeologists uncover ancient ruins in hopes of finding fabulous riches. However, archaeology is not about hidden treasure.

Professional archaeologists want to answer the questions of who, what, where, when, why, and how people in an area once lived.

66 People most often think of digging as the main activity related to archaeology, but really, for one day in the field, we spend five days back in the lab processing the materials. . . . We analyze pottery not just to figure out when it was made and by who, we also try and figure out what kind of vessel the fragment came from, how much it might have cost, and where it was purchased and shipped from. These kinds of questions lead us far beyond who lived at the site and when, to more complicated stories we can tell about how people lived in the past 99

—Sarah Miller,
director of the Northeast/East Central Region of the Florida Public Archaeology Network

As it is not possible to travel through time, archaeologists learn about what life was like through investigation and excavation. They look at objects that people used and left behind. These objects are known as artifacts.

Archaeologists look at where artifacts are found and the soil they are found in. They also consider how an object relates to other objects at the site. This is called context.

Right now, there are artifacts all around your room. Do you have books, artwork, and homework? How about a computer or a phone? What would these objects say about you in the future?

It is an archaeologist's job to analyze the clues given by artifacts. Then they put the pieces together, just as a detective would do to solve a crime.

One challenge to learning more about artifacts is that our ancestors did not always write their stories down. Today, we share information all the time through books, magazines, newspapers, diaries, the Internet, and social media. But people started keeping written records only 5,000 years ago. Human presence stretches back much longer. It might have begun as many as 6 million years ago!

In this book, you'll meet three women who have made careers in archaeology.

Chelsea Rose is a historical archaeologist with Southern Oregon University. Alexandra Jones runs Archaeology in the Community in Washington, DC. This is an organization that provides programs in archaeology to young people and encourages them to pursue careers in the field. Justine Benanty is a maritime archaeologist from New York City.

Each of these women have overcome many challenges to achieve their dreams. They have shown resilience in this rewarding professional field to become successful in their work.

Before we learn their stories, let's discover more about the science of archaeology. Let's see how this field has captured the imaginations of people for decades.

Ask & Answer

What is archaeology? How do archaeologists use artifacts to deepen our knowledge of past people and cultures?

CHAPTER 1

The History of Women in Archaeology

In movies, archaeologists dodge giant boulders while trying to grab artifacts and outwit ancient curses and gangs of villains. Modern archaeology is nothing like this. Archaeology requires hours of research and careful observation to study and interpret the past. Archaeology was not always a science. It grew out of a desire for prized objects. Just as you might collect stamps, rocks, or coins, people who lived long ago also built collections.

7

In 1925, a team of archaeologists excavating a temple complex in what is now the country of Iraq came across a curious room. Inside the room, they found half a dozen artifacts. There was the arm of a figure. There was a variety of carefully arranged clay tablets.

Mysteriously, the objects varied in age by hundreds of years. Nearby were clay drums. They were covered in ancient writing in three different languages. They appeared to be a sort of label. What was this place?

It was one of the earliest museums in the world, curated by a woman named Ennigaldi. She was the daughter of the last king of the Neo-Babylonian Empire (626–539 BCE). Ennigaldi was the high priestess of the moon god in the ancient city of Ur. Its ruins are in modern Iraq.

Ennigaldi is believed to have curated her museum, called the Museum of Ur, with items collected from the southern area of Mesopotamia. Her father, Nabonidus, was interested in the past. He is known as one of the first archaeologists. Maybe she learned from him to value ancient artifacts and to use them to learn about the history of the people who lived where the objects were found.

The princess was a very busy person—she also oversaw a school for girls!

The Museum of Ur

You can learn more about the original excavations at Ur by visiting this website. Archaeologists dug many different sites, including the Royal Cemetery. The excavations they made back then would not be allowed today, when there is more emphasis on preservation and conservation. What did archaeologists learn about daily life from remains of the dead?

Penn Museum Iraq 🔍

COLLECTING ARTIFACTS

Before there was archaeology, there was collecting. People found or bought ancient artifacts and kept them. The Renaissance was a popular time for collectors. This exciting period spanned the fourteenth to the seventeenth centuries. It was a time of almost daily discoveries, with sailors, merchants, and travelers exploring more of the world than ever before.

As the middle class grew, more people had the time to learn, invent, and create. They became fascinated with rediscovering the sculpture, architecture, and other arts, especially of ancient Greece and Rome.

As people traveled to new parts of the globe, they brought home many rare objects. Collecting became a popular hobby in Europe, especially for the wealthy and the nobility. They had the money to purchase treasures, from shells and dried seahorses to scientific instruments and art. People placed these objects in cabinets of curiosities to show to their friends.

The cabinets could be a single piece of furniture crammed with secret drawers. They could also be rooms filled to the ceiling with hundreds of objects.

Curiouser and Curiouser

Cabinets could be very elaborate pieces of furniture that were almost more interesting than the objects they contained! You can look at the detail of one cabinet of curiosity at this website. What kind of artwork do you see on the cabinet? Why do you think the artist created such intricate details for a cabinet?

Getty cabinet curiosities 🔍

One important collector during the Renaissance was Isabella d'Este Gonzaga (1474–1539). Isabella studied ancient Roman history and she learned Greek and Latin. After marrying a nobleman from Mantua, in northern Italy, Isabella devoted her time to turning the area into a cultural center.

A drawing of Isabella d'Este Gonzaga by Leonardo da Vinci

At a time when women had little opportunity, Isabella became an influential patron of poets, writers, and artists, such as Leonardo da Vinci (1452–1519). Leonard da Vinci's portrait of Isabella d'Este now hangs in the Louvre Museum in Paris.

Isabella used her position to commission paintings and collect Greek and Roman art. She became so well-respected that her family asked her advice before purchasing artwork.

As Isabella's collection grew, guidebooks written in the sixteenth century began to mention it. People traveled to Mantua to see her impressive collection of paintings, coins, engraved gems, antique bronzes, and more than 200 books.

By the eighteenth century, private collections became the basis of art and natural history museums.

Enameled mustard pots, vases, and dishes with medallions of roses interested a collector named Charlotte Schreiber (1812–1895). This was some of the rare china that she spent 15 years searching for all across Europe.

Charlotte was born in Lincolnshire, England. She loved learning and taught herself many languages, including Arabic, Hebrew, Persian, and Welsh. She also became interested in medieval life and Celtic history, translating Welsh legends into English.

After her husband's death in 1852, Charlotte remarried and began building what would become one of the finest eighteenth-century collections of china in the world. She traveled by coach and train, always "on the chase," as she called it, for the best chinaware in the world. When her second husband died, Charlotte donated 1,800 pieces of her china to the Victoria and Albert Museum in London.

COLLECTING VS. ARCHAEOLOGY

Professor Katherine Cook teaches at McMaster University in Canada and works at Sustainable Archaeology. The facility stores more than 80,000 boxes of artifacts. Some of these artifacts come from collectors and include notes explaining where and when an object was found. Many objects do not come with a clear context.

Ask & Answer

Have you ever collected stamps, coins, or rocks? What did you learn from your collection? If you were to start a new collection, what would it be and why? How would you share this collection with family and friends?

According to Katherine, a few collectors have even used their own secret code to write down context to prevent others from locating similar artifacts! This makes the job of discovering where an artifact came from more difficult.

At the facility, archaeologists must be creative. They spend hours going through files at donors' homes. They also turn to social media to track down retired archaeologists associated with some of these objects.

Katharine says, "One of the important things that separates archaeology from collecting is the value placed on context, but, unfortunately, there is a very long history of people collecting. So many people are interested in the past, but if they aren't careful, they end up erasing the past, rather than preserving it."

The importance of context in archaeology is evident when we consider one of the first archaeological sites to be discovered. The Roman town of Herculaneum was buried under ash, mud, and other material when Mount Vesuvius erupted on August 24, 79 CE. The eruption also buried the town of Pompeii in ash.

In 1709, treasure hunters began digging tunnels through the 75 feet of material to reach Herculaneum. They found rare marble, statues, and beautiful paintings called frescos, some with images of Greek goddesses.

The ruins of Pompeii with Mount Vesuvius in the distance

Later, in 1763, Pompeii was rediscovered. It became a huge sensation, with artists taking inspiration from its architecture and art.

Caroline Bonaparte Murat (1782–1839) took an interest in the ruins of Pompeii. Caroline was the sister of Napoleon Bonaparte, who at that time ruled France and much of Europe. In 1808, her husband became the king of Naples, Italy.

After coming to power, Caroline organized a show to present the treasures of Pompeii to the public. However, they were disappointed that many treasures had already been taken away by collectors. This inspired them to pass a law in 1807 that made it illegal to ship antiquities abroad.

Caroline then began to oversee the excavations in Pompeii. She hoped that her workers would locate the original city walls. Though Caroline was unable to see the project through after her brother was overthrown, she did succeed in placing some objects from Pompeii in the Royal Portici Museum.

PIONEERING WOMEN IN ARCHAEOLOGY

The earliest archaeologists did not know how far back human culture went. In the eighteenth century, some scientists began questioning how old the earth was. Once people realized that the earth was older than previously thought, archaeologists began to look further into the past.

Ask & Answer

Today, modern archaeologists often do not excavate an entire site but investigate only a portion of it. Imagine that you have been asked to investigate a historical site near you, which has written records. How would records, including diaries and newspapers, help you in your investigation?

Cool Careers:
Garden Archaeologist

Wilhelmina Jashemski (1910–2007) was an archaeologist who established the field of garden archaeology. Two centuries after Pompeii was rediscovered, Wilhelmina began her pioneering work at the site. She made plaster casts of roots, which botanists then studied.

Wilhelmina discovered how gardens were important to everyday life in Pompeii. She learned that gardens were not only used to grow vines, fruits, and flowers, but were also sites for religious activities. Wilhelmina's findings allowed people to see the connections between ancient people and their natural and built environments.

Today, garden archaeologists carefully excavate and reconstruct ancient gardens to learn what people planted, how they designed the landscape, and to discover what purposes these gardens served.

During the following decades, the field of archaeology rapidly expanded. There were developments in how objects should be dated and how sites were excavated and studied. There were many discoveries of previously unknown civilizations.

As the study of archaeology grew in the nineteenth century, women began making more contributions to the field. They initiated excavations and surveyed sites around the world. They wrote papers and books on their findings and lectured on their experiences. They raised money for the preservation and study of sites.

The achievements of these women are even more extraordinary because education and opportunities were not always equal for men and women. These women were determined to work in archaeology. They did not wait for someone to open the door for them—they pushed right through it! The careers of the following archaeologists represent only a few of those women.

In 1873, writer Amelia Edwards (1831–1892) set sail up the Nile to Abu Simbel, an ancient site in Egypt known for its massive rock temples carved into a sandstone cliff. During her travels, Amelia became deeply concerned about the state of Egypt's ruins.

She found broken slabs and fragments of columns. The damage was not the consequence of time, but of treasure hunters. She worried about the affects of tourism and modern urbanization on sites.

Amelia's Egyptian trip was the beginning of a new career for her as an Egyptologist. She became determined to read hieroglyphics, and studied them until she could understand their meanings. She wrote about Egypt for academic journals. She lectured in England and in North America to raise awareness of the need to preserve and study ancient Egyptian sites and artifacts before they vanished.

Illustrating Archaeology

Amelia Edwards illustrated many of her own books with drawings she made of the things she saw on her travels. You can view her sketches at this website. Now, many archaeologists use photographs to document their travels and excavations. Do you think one medium is better than the other? Why? What are the benefits of each?

Amelia Edwards Griffith 🔍

A drawing by Amelia Edwards of statues at Abu Simbel
(PD-US)

Her book *A Thousand Miles Up the Nile* was based on her three-month Nile journey. It played an important role in raising the issue of protecting monuments.

In 1882, Amelia helped found the Egypt Exploration Fund (now called the Egypt Exploration Society) to support excavations and research in Egypt and Sudan. Because of Amelia's work, the study of ancient Egyptian history grew.

In 1892, she left her entire collection of ancient Egyptian artifacts, including bronzes, statues, and vases to University College London. This collection became the foundation for the college's Egyptology department.

In 1881, French archaeologist Jane Dieulafoy (1851–1916) accompanied her husband, Marcel, to Persia to study monuments. Jane had a talent for writing, drawing, and learning languages. She used these skills during the couple's travels in Persia to keep a detailed diary filled with notes and photographs of the trip.

Jane was a pioneer in her use of photography to record archaeological sites. During her time, sketching was the most popular method of recording sites. She helped show the world actual images of sites many people would never get to see in person.

The Dieulafoys returned to Persia in 1884. They were part of a team excavating the ancient city of Susa, north of the Persian Gulf. On her first night at Susa, Jane wrote, "To have reached the soil Susa, to encamp on the ruins of the palaces of the great kings, is that not already a victory?"

Jane often dressed as a man and kept her hair short when she traveled. She thought it was easier to do her work if people mistook her for a boy.

(PD-US)

During the Susa excavations, the Dieulafoys unearthed a massive capital, or the top of a column. It had once been part of 36 columns that measured a staggering 68 feet in height. The columns formed the hall of a royal palace dating to about 510 BCE. The Dieulafoys brought the capital back to France, where Jane organized an exhibition of objects from Susa. The objects were shown at a museum in Paris called the Louvre. Officials at the museum later decided to name two rooms in her honor.

Jane gave lectures and published her journals in *Le Tour du Monde* from 1883 to 1886. Two years later, they were published as a book called *Á Suse, Journal des Fouilles, 1884–1886* (*At Suse: Journal of the Excavations, 1884–1886*). The French government recognized Jane's work in Persia. In 1886, she received the Legion of Honor, the French government's highest award.

Gertrude Bell (1868–1926) was another archaeologist who was deeply interested in the Middle East. In 1886, Gertrude became the first woman to earn an honors degree in modern history from Oxford University, England.

66 The gates of the enclosed garden are thrown open, the chain at the entrance of the sanctuary is lowered, with a wary glance to right and left you step forth, and behold! The immeasurable world. 99

—Gertrude Bell,
writer and explorer

Letters Home

You can read Gertrude Bell's letters and diaries online. Because there was no email or social media back then, letters and diaries are a good way for archaeologists and historians to learn about what life was like in the past. Do you think in the future historians will read emails from today to learn about your life and culture? Are there different challenges about email than there are for letters?

Gertrude Bell archive 🔍

At the age of 23, after studying Persian, Gertrude went to Tehran, Persia. Her uncle was the British ambassador to Persia. Gertrude traveled first on the *Orient Express* train to Constantinople, or modern-day Istanbul, and then by boat to Persia. In letters home, she described Persia as a paradise. In 1894, Gertrude published her impressions of the trip in a travel book called *Persian Pictures*.

During the next 10 years, Gertrude traveled the world and pursued an interest in archaeological work. She researched sites across the Syrian Desert to Asia Minor. These included the first scientific study of a magnificent walled palace called the Al-Ukhaidir Fortress in Iraq.

A photo Gertrude took of her team of workers in Turkey, 1907.
(PD-US)

Gertrude took hundreds of photographs and made notes on her travels and about local customs. She published her observations and studies in papers and travel books such as *The Desert and the Sown*.

In 1913, Gertrude received a prestigious medal from the Royal Geographical Society for her archaeological work. After World War I (1914–1918), Gertrude's interest in archaeology led her to Iraq. She wrote the first Iraqi laws to prevent the country's artifacts from being looted by treasure hunters. Gertrude also founded the Baghdad Archaeological Museum. She held the position of honorary director of antiquities there until her death in 1926.

Harriet Boyd Hawes (1871–1945) was another famous archaeologist. After studying classics at Smith College in Massachusetts, she enrolled at the American School of Classical Studies at Athens in 1896.

Harriet was eager to learn about the archaeology and history of Greece. She wanted to participate in excavations, but her professors advised her to concentrate on research. Women were still often discouraged from fieldwork. However, Harriet was not going to take no for an answer. She wanted the opportunity to visit and work at archaeological sites all around Greece.

In the spring of 1900, Harriet arrived on the island of Crete and began work. Relatively few women traveled by themselves at this time and fewer still ran excavations. After starting work on the eastern side of the island, Harriet found houses and tombs dating to 900 BCE.

Comic Art

PS

Newcastle University in the United Kingdom created a comic series based on events from Gertrude's remarkable life. You can learn more about this dynamic woman by visiting this website.

What do you notice about how the comic pages are organized? How could you communicate the same information using a different format?

Gertrude Bell comics 🔍

One year later, Harriet began work on a nearby site called Gournia. She hired and organized a crew of 100 people to excavate the site. What emerged from her labor was an entire town that dated to the early Bronze Age, about 1500 BCE. Because of Harriet's work, people learned more about the lives and habits of people in ancient Crete.

Later, Harriet became the first woman invited to speak at the Archaeological Institute of America (AIA). She lectured on her experiences in Crete to 10 different AIA branches. Harriet went on to teach at Wellesley College in Massachusetts until 1936.

Mary Douglas Leakey (1913–1996) was an archaeologist and paleoanthropologist. Her interest in archaeology began when she was a young child exploring cave paintings in France.

The Gournia Site

Harriet Boyd's work continues today at the Gournia site on Crete. How do you think the excavations done there today differ from the work Harriet oversaw more than 100 years ago? To learn more, visit this website.

Gournia excavation 🔍

At the age of 17, she started working as an assistant to archaeologist Dorothy Liddell on an Iron Age fort in England.

Mary had a gift for illustration and drawing and made sketches of artifacts from the site. She also began attending lectures at University College London to learn more about archaeology. Later, Mary studied with other archaeologists in Africa, where she gained knowledge of Paleolithic sites and the tools humans used during the Stone Age.

After she married scientist Louis Leakey in the 1930s, the couple began excavating prehistoric sites together in Kenya and Tanzania. In 1948, Mary Leakey made the first of many incredible discoveries. She found fragments of a skull and jaws of a new species of primate that lived 14 to 23 million years ago. Humans are primates, as are apes, monkeys, and chimpanzees. It was the first time such a skull had ever been found!

Ask & Answer

Using a Venn diagram, compare and contrast drawing and photography. Think about reasons why archaeologists record their findings and how they could use these images.

When Mary returned to London, everyone wanted to know more about this important find.

In 1959, Mary discovered a human fossil that was about 1.75 million years old. She assembled the 400 pieces into an almost complete skull. The discovery was very important because it showed that human culture was older than people had thought.

After her husband died, Mary continued working in Africa. In 1978, she found human footprints that dated to about 3.5 million years ago. They showed two humans walking side by side. This suggested that humans began walking on two legs much earlier than anyone in the scientific community had believed.

Mary worked until the 1980s. During her lifetime, she received many awards for her work, including the National Geographic Society's highest honor, the Hubbard Award.

In the decades since the accomplishments of these women, thousands of other talented women have entered archaeology. They are engaged in a variety of different jobs.

Ask & Answer

Why is it important for women to have the same career opportunities as men?

Women lead and plan excavations. They introduce the public to archaeology through community programs. They teach at universities and conduct research around the globe. In labs full of pottery, bones, and bits of metal, they sort, classify, and label.

Without these women, it would not be possible to learn and preserve human culture or understand its impact on the future.

CAREERS IN ARCHAEOLOGY

If you are interested in the past and enjoy solving mysteries, maybe you would make a good archaeologist. Archaeology combines many subjects. Archaeologists need to know about history, geography, science, mathematics, and art. They often take classes in anthropology to learn about people throughout the world.

College students can also enroll in classical languages or biology, depending on their specific interests. Archaeology majors gain experience by analyzing and cataloguing artifacts in research labs.

In addition to work done in the classroom, students develop skills at field schools. Field schools are short-term work experiences in which students learn to survey, map, dig, and document.

These field school experiences could include a study of a seventeenth-century farmstead or a fort from the American Civil War (1861–1865). It might be an analysis of a 2,000-year-old rice terrace in the Philippines.

After completing their college degree, graduates might find work as archivists, archaeological assistants, or as field technicians. Field technicians are people who take notes, dig, clean, sort, and catalog objects on site.

However, many management, teaching, and research positions require graduate degrees. At graduate school, students specialize in a branch of archaeology and work on projects based on original research.

Ask & Answer

Archaeologists conduct research before, during, and after a dig. A report done by the Canadian government suggested that archaeologists spend 10 minutes doing paperwork for every minute they dig. What do you think are the benefits of record keeping during and after a dig? How would a person use these records in the future?

Classical archaeologists, for example, become experts on civilizations such as the Greeks and the Romans. Historical archaeologists study cultures that have written records. Mostly, they focus on the modern world.

Maritime archaeologists investigate what people left behind under the water. This might be ancient or modern wrecks or underwater villages. Prehistoric archaeologists investigate the world before there was writing.

In this book, you will learn about many female archaeologists, including Monica Hanna, Gertrude Caton-Thompson, and Kristina Killgrove. Their work will allow you to see what it means to be an archaeologist.

Plus, you will meet three women who will explain what inspired them to pursue their careers and the exciting opportunities their work has brought them. They will also share how they use their archaeological training to record, search, and study the past. And you'll read how they are sharing their knowledge of archaeology with curious students just like you.

Chelsea Rose is an archaeologist with the Southern Oregon University Laboratory of Anthropology. She specializes in the archaeology of the Old West and works on many public archaeological projects in Oregon.

Alexandra Jones is the founder and director of the nonprofit organization Archaeology in the Community, Washington, DC. She engages young people and the public in the exploration of the past to develop an appreciation for archaeology.

Justine Benanty is a maritime archaeologist whose adventures lead her to underwater antiquities and their management. She reaches the public through her company, ArchaeoVenturers, which uses virtual media and encourages young people to learn about maritime conservation through Youth Diving with a Purpose.

Maybe one of these women will inspire you to pursue a career in archaeology!

66 I especially appreciated the different components of archaeology—excavation, studying materials, architectural analysis, survey, ground-penetrating radar, paleoethnobotany, zooarchaeology—that archaeologists could use and combine for their studies. **99**

—Caroline Cheung,
PhD candidate in the ancient history and Mediterranean archaeology department at the University of California, Berkeley

CHAPTER TWO
Chelsea Rose

Chelsea Rose is a historical archaeologist and researcher at the Southern Oregon University Laboratory of Anthropology (SOULA), where she studies towns and mining camps of the Gold Rush era. For two seasons, she was a member of *Time Team America*, a popular television show about archaeological digs. Chelsea enjoys telling the stories of people who have been neglected in the history books. She is passionate about bringing their stories back to life.

For the past decade, Chelsea's enthusiasm for archaeology has been inspiring entire communities and young people across the United States to explore their shared past. "Archaeology is such a cool career," says Chelsea. "It is a blend of all of my favorite things—adventure, books, and mysteries!"

Chelsea is from northern California. She grew up near the Sierra Nevada Mountains before coming to Oregon as a teenager. From a young age, she expressed an interest in history and archaeology. Chelsea always had an urge to explore.

The Sierras were a good place for her to be as a child. She loved being surrounded by local archaeological sites. These sites date from prehistoric times to the first European settlement of the West. It was a perfect area for a curious child, and Chelsea was very curious. She could roam and learn all year long.

Lava Beds National Monument
photo credit: National Park Service

Kintpuash, also known as Captain Jack, was chief of a Modoc tribe. He was the leader of a band during the Modoc War of 1872–1873 that held off the U.S. Army in the lava bed area of California for months. This photo was taken after he was captured.

photo credit: National Archive

One of Chelsea's favorite activities with her family was to step back in time at the Lava Beds National Monument in California. At the lava beds, she was fascinated by the network of trenches and rock outcrops that make up the natural lava fortress called Captain Jack's Stronghold.

Chelsea was also drawn to the awe-inspiring rock art of the Modoc people and those who came before them. Some of these images are more than 6,000 years old! Who were the Native American artists who carved these images into the lava beds? What did these images mean? How were they made? Chelsea's family encouraged her interest in the past by visiting the area.

Visit the Lava Beds

The Lava Beds National Monument is home to two types of rock art—petroglyphs, which are carvings, and painted pictographs. Some of the images might be as old as 6,000 years old. You can explore the lava beds through descriptions and photos at this website. Why is it important to protect ancient rock art?

rock art lava beds 🔍

Ghost towns also captured Chelsea's imagination. The Sierra Nevadas have many abandoned mining towns deep in the mountains, such as the town of Bodie. This town flourished for a few years in the late 1800s before being abandoned. Today, its buildings remain as they were when the last residents left more than 50 years ago.

However, Chelsea's favorite historical town was not in California. Virginia City, Nevada, was a pioneering town built in the 1800s. It was once filled with trappers, miners, homesteaders, and ranchers. Today, there are stagecoaches to ride in, mansions to peer into, and mines to tour. Chelsea thought that it was the coolest place to be. "I would have preferred it to Disneyland any day!" she says.

Bodie, California

Chelsea's interest in history grew to include places farther away. She developed a strong interest in Egyptology. Her father took her to see the largest collection of Egyptian artifacts in western North America at the Rosicrucian Egyptian Museum in San Jose, California.

The experience had a big effect on Chelsea. When she was 10, she declared her love for pyramids, mummies, and all things Egypt in a poem. The following poem was published in an anthology of children's poetry.

> 66 I love the old buildings, so old and tall,
> And the ancient writing that covers the wall.
> Maybe Egypt's not quite what it seems,
> but who cares, those are my dreams. 99

—Chelsea Rose

SCHOOL DECISIONS

Chelsea continued to study history in high school. She was also interested in art. At this time, Chelsea did not pursue math or the sciences. She was never discouraged from studying these subjects, but she was more interested in art and history.

Chelsea earned a reputation for being creative. As a young person, Chelsea saw this label as a negative observation about her science skills, though it may not have been meant this way.

The label made Chelsea believe that she was better in the arts than in the sciences. When she was older, she grew to understand that "you can do both. Science is a very creative process!"

Chelsea's interests led her to the University of Oregon (U of O), where she studied anthropology. The program at the U of O is divided into three main areas of focus—archaeology, biological anthropology, and cultural anthropology.

Chelsea stayed at the school for only two semesters. She was concerned about her future. Though she liked the program at the U of O, she was not convinced that a career in archaeology was for her.

Like many young undergraduates, she was unsure if she "could commit to focusing on one thing for the rest of my life," she says. Due to these concerns, Chelsea took some time away from school. Now, Chelsea wonders if perhaps she was simply in a rush to get out of school so she could travel.

After leaving school, Chelsea had the chance to travel to places that she had never visited before. She hiked across the vast Australian Outback. She once got lost in the Carpathian Mountains of Slovakia. She ate giant pretzels in Bavaria. Closer to home, she camped on beaches in Mexico.

Of course, all this travel required money. Chelsea did many different jobs to pay for it. She used her art skills to make jewelry. She sold Turkish coffee. She also built straw-bale homes and started an organic farm!

Eventually, Chelsea thought more about her future. She tried to imagine what she would be doing in five years' time. The answer was archaeology. She made the decision to go back to the U of O.

It was not until much later that Chelsea realized that those experiences she had during her absence from school shaped the person she became. Because of her experiences, she became a better anthropologist and, later, an archaeologist.

Chelsea Rose traveling in Alaska

BECOMING AN ARCHAEOLOGIST

Chelsea's appetite for new experiences continued to motivate her after she made the decision to complete her studies. She found opportunities even while driving.

Chelsea had never been shy. If she had been, she would never have found her first archaeological job. One day, Chelsea saw people working by the side of the road. They were conducting an archaeological dig in the historic mining town of Jacksonville, Oregon. Chelsea had to pull over. She promptly introduced herself.

As it turned out, the team was with the University of Oregon Museum of Natural and Cultural History. They were excavating a part of Jacksonville's Chinatown. Chelsea was given permission to participate in the excavation. She admits that perhaps the team did not know what to make of her.

In the beginning, Chelsea mostly helped look for small artifacts by using a screen. After Chelsea had been with the project for some time, she progressed to other jobs. She helped clean and analyze objects. By the time Chelsea was back in school full-time, she was "totally hooked" on archaeology.

Screening

Archaeologists use screens to sift soil from a trench that they are excavating. Most screens sit on a box, which rests on a tripod. Archaeologists place soil from a trench on top of the screen. They gently rock the screen back and forth. Soil pours through the screen. If there are any artifacts in the soil, they will remain above the screen and be freed from the dirt.

As a result of her initiative, Chelsea ended up working for the University of Oregon's Museum of Natural and Cultural History for several years. Chelsea says that she is "very thankful they were willing to give me a chance. My life changed that day. I can't imagine where I would be if I had taken a different route home!"

A GOLD RUSH TOWN

After finishing her undergraduate studies, Chelsea continued her education at Sonoma State University in California. She enrolled in a master's program in cultural resources management (CRM). In this program, students such as Chelsea are trained to protect, preserve, and manage cultural resources. These include historic sites, buildings, structures, and landscapes.

Chelsea describes the role of a CRM, saying that it is their job to go and see "where archaeological sites are, if they are important, and, if they are, how we can preserve them. If they can't be left in place, we excavate them to save the information they contain."

As part of Chelsea's program, she was required to complete an original piece of research and write a report called a thesis based on her data. Chelsea was fascinated by the Gold Rush period of Oregon. Oregon's Gold Rush began during the 1850s.

Chelsea decided to focus her investigation on the mining camp of Kanaka Flat. The camp was about a mile from Jacksonville and where some of Oregon's earliest gold discoveries occurred. There were many myths associated with the town. Stories circulated that Kanaka Flat had been a rowdy gold mining camp of miners.

During the Gold Rush, a large population of Native Hawaiians had lived there. Yet, little was known about their daily life at the camp.

There were many questions for Chelsea to pursue. Who were the people who lived there? How had they lived? Did they have families? Was Kanaka Flat really a violent place during the Gold Rush? Chelsea was determined to tell their story.

Miners during the Gold Rush

Chelsea used census records, mining claims, and newspapers to create a picture of the community. She conducted research at various institutions, including the U of O and the Oregon Historical Society. She interviewed current residents of the area to learn more about the stereotypes associated with the camp's history.

Chelsea was able to show that Kanaka Flats had been a community of families. According to the records, Portuguese, Hawaiian, and Native American miners lived at the camp. Local history, which was primarily written by European Americans, had ignored these minority miners.

Kanaka Flat

You can read a newspaper article about Chelsea's work on the Kanaka Flat at this site. Why is it important to look beyond stereotypes when learning history? How can cultural bias affect the way we understand history?

Mail Tribune Kanaka Flat 🔍

Chelsea's project uncovered the forgotten story of Kanaka Flat. It also highlighted the need for more research into towns and mining camps of the Old West. How many more stories are there to tell? Only archaeology will be able to answer this question.

WORKING IN THE MEDIA

Shortly after graduating from Sonoma State University, the television show *Time Team America* hired Chelsea. Chelsea had worked with one of the program's archaeologists, Dr. Julie Schablitsky, on sites in Oregon and Scotland. Julie thought that Chelsea would fit onto the team.

Ask & Answer

Why is it important to study different cultures from different points of view?

Chelsea became the program's lead excavator. It was an exciting opportunity for her. Chelsea says of the experience, "I got to meet such great archaeologists from across the nation, visit some of the coolest sites, and be a part of something that helped teach people about archaeology."

Chelsea led excavation work at different sites, including Camp Lawton in Georgia. By the end of the American Civil War, nearly 10,000 Union prisoners were held at the camp. But during the following decades, the exact location of the camp had been lost. Then, in 2009, archaeologists with Georgia Southern University found evidence of the prison camp. They invited *Time Team* to excavate the site.

It was Chelsea's job to help discover the original site. Records showed that there was a Confederate fort, prison towers, and officer quarters. Would Chelsea's excavations reveal evidence of these areas? Chelsea and her colleagues worked with a group of about 40 volunteer archaeologists and students from Georgia Southern University.

Students mapped the investigation site where artifacts had been discovered in 2009. They created a grid with string and pegs hammered into the ground. Excavations within what archaeologists believe was the prison area revealed a remarkable find.

They unearthed a brass picture frame. It was the type of frame that a man would have carried in his pocket with a photo of his loved one from home. The frame was a deeply personal item. It made Chelsea think about this man and his plight. Did he ever return home to his family? Her fascination with this object is part of what makes Chelsea a good archaeologist.

Chelsea continues to work with the media to make archaeology more accessible to people. She writes blog posts and newspaper articles. She gives lectures to the public. Chelsea appears on radio programs and YouTube archaeological channels with the goal of reminding people that archaeology is about them.

66 Archeology is the study of humanity itself, and unless that attitude toward the subject is kept in mind, archaeology will be overwhelmed by impossible theories or a welter of flint chips. 99

—Margaret Murray (1863–1963),
Egyptologist and anthropologist

Cool Careers: **Bioarchaeologist**

Also known as an osteoarchaeologist, a bioarchaeologist studies human remains found in archaeological sites. There is a lot you can learn from a body! You can learn what people ate, how they moved around, what their health and habits were like, and a bit about their lifestyles. Bioarchaeologists study teeth, other parts of the skeleton, any hair that is still left, and anything else that remains of a body. They can discover what sort of stress the person encountered when they were alive, whether it was hunger, injuries, or workload.

CHINATOWN

In Oregon, Chelsea has been busy working on several archaeological sites. One site presented Chelsea with the opportunity to learn more about the Chinese community in Oregon in the nineteenth century.

For the past several years, Chelsea has led a dig in Jacksonville's Chinese Quarter. The Chinese Quarter was established in the mid-1850s. Chelsea knew what she was excavating, but the site still held a surprise. She found "the perfectly preserved remains of a burned-down house!"

Chelsea's archaeology site was not hidden from residents. It was out in the open. The house was off Jacksonville's main street. Schoolchildren were able to check her progress. One lucky pair of kids saw an artifact that no one else had set eyes upon since the fire in 1888!

On the excavation, Chelsea did not work alone, but with a team of skilled people. Chelsea explains, "Not only do the excavations require teamwork, but the best work is collaborative, and builds off of the insight and knowledge of many people."

By 2015, Chelsea's team had nearly finished their analysis at the SOULA lab of a staggering 30,000 artifacts, including dishes, games, clothing, bones, and seeds and plants from the site.

From this information, Chelsea created a vibrant picture of Jacksonville's Chinese residents in the 1880s. Up until then, their stories had not been explained in the same detail as stories of other settlers to Jacksonville.

Ask & Answer

What does teamwork mean to you? Give an example of a time when you worked on a project with several other people. What was it like?

Because of Chelsea's commitment to community archaeology, she included Jacksonville's citizens in this archaeological experience. Community volunteers aided in the excavation. And the two curious students who had followed Chelsea's progress entered the trench on the last day, after everything had been recorded. What an exciting experience!

Kristina Killgrove

Dr. Kristina Killgrove is a bioarchaeologist who has been studying the remains of 200 Roman skeletons for the past decade. She explains, "We know a lot about them [Romans] from the written history they left behind, of course, but not very much about the average person living in Rome. I like to ask questions about what life was like for women and children in Rome, or for people who moved to Rome from far away, because ancient historians didn't think these questions were very interesting."

She first looks at the skeletons for clues about their sex or evidence of disease. She then uses measuring tapes, rulers, and calipers to determine their height and chemistry to learn what chemicals make up their bones.

AN EYE TO THE FUTURE

At present, Chelsea is exploring archaeological sites in the United States. When she is not on the road excavating or hosting public days at excavation sites, she is busy examining and cataloging artifacts at Southern Oregon University's Laboratory of Anthropology.

These tests reveal what they ate, where they were born, and how they died.

Kristina has learned that Romans "came from parts of Europe, Africa, and Asia. They're all unique in what they were eating, what diseases they had, and the shapes of their bodies. I've learned that there really is no 'typical Roman!'"

To learn more about Kristina's work, visit this weblink.

Roman DNA project 🔎

Check It Out on YouTube

You can see Chelsea Rose talk about the work she and her team did in Georgia at Camp Lawton here. What are some of the tools they used to learn about the history of this place? Why is it important to consider the history of a place within a context? What was the context of the picture frame that she found there?

Chelsea Rose Camp Lawton video

Archaeologists are always working hard, says Chelsea. They need to identify, investigate, and preserve the past. Where are they conducting this work? It might be right near you! If you want to help them, Chelsea says, "You can reach out to your state's historic preservation office and find a way to volunteer and get involved. Better yet, become an archaeologist and help us preserve these sites for the future!"

When she was younger, Chelsea doubted herself. She thought that because she was creative, she might not make a good scientist. But she soon realized that scientists are creative thinkers.

Chelsea says, "Everyone's experiences allow them to see the world in a slightly different way, and that is a good thing. Archaeology, just like any science, needs fresh ideas and new perspectives to keep it moving forward."

CHAPTER THREE
Alexandra Jones

Dr. Alexandra Jones specializes in community archaeology. She develops exciting programs that encourage everyone to experience archaeology. The founder of a nonprofit organization in Washington, DC, called Archaeology in the Community (AITC), she also teaches anthropology at the University of Baltimore. For more than a decade, Alexandra has been introducing young people to archaeology through her unique, hands-on programs that teach kids how to discover.

Alexandra grew up in Washington, DC. With a mother who worked at the Smithsonian, Alexandra's life hummed with discussions on history and culture. Throughout her childhood, Alexandra spent a lot of time at museums and was fortunate to be able to attend special events. These experiences fed Alexandra's interest in learning more about people from all around the globe.

As Alexandra grew up, she thought about how she could help others. She began to take an interest in medicine and enrolled in advanced placement classes in high school with the goal of being a doctor.

Alexandra pursued these interests at Howard University in Washington, DC. She was the third generation of her family to attend Howard. She initially planned to seek a double major in history and biology. However, her biology class proved to be an obstacle to achieving her goal—her grades weren't high enough to pass.

Determined, she retook the class, but the result was the same. Her mother suggested a new path. She encouraged Alexandra to study anthropology instead. She explained to Alexandra that anthropology would enable her to explore history and science.

Alexandra tried not to be discouraged. She took her mother's advice and enrolled in anthropology classes. Where would it lead her?

Her new course of study allowed Alexandra to cover four major fields of anthropology—linguistic anthropology, cultural anthropology, physical (biological) anthropology, and archaeology.

In her first anthropology class, a well-respected researcher, Dr. Bruce Dahlin, taught about Maya archaeology. The ancient Maya created one of the greatest civilizations in Mesoamerica around 2600 BCE. This is a large cultural region. It spanned central Mexico to areas of Guatemala, Belize, Honduras, and El Salvador. The Maya built magnificent stone cities, some with thousands of structures, including temple-pyramids.

Alexandra enjoyed the course so much that she found herself looking forward to it each week. She was soon hooked on the subject. She says, "I remember sitting in my first cultural anthropology class and thinking, bingo, this is what I want to do with my life. I am a people person, and I love to meet, learn about, and learn from other people."

Ask & Answer

Why do you think that it is important to set goals? On a piece of paper, write down one of your goals. Next, write down three simple steps to take to help you achieve this goal.

Alexandra learned of an exciting opportunity for fieldwork. Every year, the professor took students to a large ancient Maya site on the Yucatán Peninsula in southeastern Mexico. The archaeological project offered students the chance to join a team of professional archaeologists. The idea of taking part in an actual field experience, combined with the opportunity to work with the Maya people who still live in the region, greatly appealed to Alexandra. She could not let this opportunity slip away!

Alexandra worked hard to secure a place on the trip. She met regularly with her professor. She even volunteered for extra credit, reading site reports on the archaeological dig in the Yucatán.

In archaeology, a site report is a descriptive record of a site that includes pictures and drawings. It also includes information such as the location, size, and features of a site. Alexandra received an A in the class and a spot on the trip! She was on her way to becoming an archaeologist.

Ask & Answer

Think about a field trip that you enjoyed and the hands-on activities that you participated in. How did these activities change your knowledge of the subject that you were studying? Why are hands-on activities useful when learning about a topic?

Meet the Maya

Xocnacah is an ancient Maya city that archaeological groups have excavated and where they have discovered fascinating things. In this video, you can see a huge platform being unearthed, along with a reconstruction of what the plaza on top might have looked like.

PBS learning quest for lost Maya 🔍

FIRST DIG

In the summer after her first year, Alexandra flew to Mexico. This was not only Alexandra's first dig, but her first experience out of the United States. Alexandra did not know what to expect, but she was very excited.

Her adventure began as soon as she hit the ground. After being picked up by her professor in an old jeep, they drove for hours. She had only the vaguest idea of where she was going. Alexandra did not say a word the entire drive, She explains that she "was so busy taking everything in and enjoying the sights."

When she finally arrived at her lodgings, it was already dark. Where was she? She was at the site of Chunchucmil. More than 1,500 years ago, this was a major center of the Maya.

During the following weeks, Alexandra and her fellow archaeologists investigated how the ancient Maya people lived. Like all archaeological investigations, this one began with a question. The team wanted to know if the Maya had turned to trading goods and services for food after years of drought.

The days were long and hot. The showers were cold and the horseflies were hungry. But Alexandra loved it all. In fact, it was awesome! She was glad to work on the Maya and learn more about the culture first-hand. By the end of the field school, Alexandra had fallen in love with archaeology.

MAKING A DREAM HAPPEN

In 2001, Alexandra completed her bachelor of arts degree in history and anthropology from Howard. Yet, she was unsure of the direction her life would take. Alexandra longed to pursue archaeology, but she wondered if this was a wise decision. Many questions swirled around her. Were there jobs in the field and would she find one?

Alexandra took a chance. She applied to a graduate program in archaeology. But her dream hit a road bump. Unfortunately, Alexandra did not get into an archaeology department that she wanted to study in.

Alexandra quickly changed course. She decided to pursue a master of arts in history at Howard with a minor in secondary education. Alexandra thought that perhaps this graduate degree would lead to a career in teaching social studies to middle-grade students.

During the next two years, Alexandra not only went to school full-time but also worked as a sixth-grade teacher. Teaching came naturally to her. However, Alexandra felt that something was missing in her life. "Deep down," says Alexandra, "I really wanted to pursue a career in archaeology."

Alexandra decided to "go for it." She reapplied to graduate school to study archaeology and her determination paid off. She was accepted into the University of California, Berkeley.

She was going to pursue her dream.

Ask & Answer

Why do you think it is important to follow your dreams? Who in your life has encouraged you to dream bigger?

FOLLOWING HER DREAM

In 2003, Alexandra began graduate studies at Berkeley. As part of her PhD, she was required to do original research. She began work with the First Agape A.M.E. (African Methodist Episcopal) Zion Church in Cabin John, Maryland.

In 1898, free African Americans had established a church here. They built it from logs. It was originally called the Gibson Grove A.M.E. Zion Church.

A newer structure, built in 1923, was the oldest African American church in the community until a fire destroyed the interior in 2004. The congregation wanted to rebuild, but the state required an archaeological survey. It was thought that there might be unmarked graves on the property. Unfortunately, the church had no money for excavation.

Alexandra and a colleague volunteered their services. The community played an important role in Alexandra's project. Alexandra gathered information in the Maryland State Archives to better understand the history of the church. She supplemented her research by interviewing descendants of people who were linked to the site.

When it was time to begin excavations, Alexandra recruited volunteers to make the task of cleaning up the site and surveying it easier. "Many hands make lighter work," Alexandra says.

Total Station

A total station is a surveying instrument used by archaeologists. The machine provides them with measurement data on distances, heights, and angles. This data is then used to create a site map.

A total station looks like a large camera. It sits on a tall tripod. The camera instrument sends out an invisible laser beam across a site to the target. The target is a rod with a prism, called a pogo. A second archaeologist working on the project holds the pogo out on the site. The laser beam hits the prism and bounces back into the total station. A computer within the machine calculates the amount of time it takes for the beam to bounce back. It uses the difference in time to calculate the distance from the station to the rod.

The machine is so accurate that it can calculate angles and distance measurements down to the millimeter. The detailed map that the total station creates helps archaeologists plot where they find artifacts and the artifacts' positions within the entire site.

Some volunteers were retired archaeologists. They came from a local chapter of the Archaeological Society of Maryland.

Alexandra also created opportunities for young people by inviting students from Montgomery County's High School Archaeology Club to join her. Alexandra taught the students how to use a cool surveying tool called a total station to create a site map.

When Alexandra completed her work, she wrote a report based on her findings. Her research revealed the history of the African American community in Cabin John. Alexandra says of the experience, "I really enjoyed the project, but the best part was being able to tell the story of an African American community that had previously been ignored."

COMMUNITY OUTREACH

During her first semester, Alexandra participated in an outreach program with Berkeley. She volunteered in a middle-grade classroom. Alexandra had always been interested in helping people. She introduced the excited students to archaeology through a mock dig.

Inspired by her participation in the outreach program, Alexandra went to speak with her advisor at Berkeley. She had an idea for another project.

Alexandra explained that her community back in Washington, DC, could benefit from a similar program. Her advisor supported Alexandra's idea and gave her the funds for her first outreach program.

Whenever Alexander returned home to Washington, DC, she conducted research with local schools. After Alexandra had offered her AITC (Archaeology in the Community) program once, the demand grew. At last, Alexandra's dream of showing young people what archaeology was all about had come true.

REACHING THE COMMUNITY

Alexandra continues to run AITC. Her work focuses on three main areas. The first provides archaeological experiences for youth. In Alexandra's after-school programs, camps, and week-long programs, children ages 5 to 14 learn about the history of archaeology and experience what an archaeologist does.

Ask & Answer

Is there something you want to be learning while you're a kid that is missing from your education? How can you make that learning happen?

Alexandra Jones teaching screening technique

Her students learn to survey and create maps. They participate in mock digs, where they carefully pull away the layers of soil to reveal artifacts. They also have the opportunity to research, write, and present their findings to their peers.

Every year, AITC hosts the Day of Archaeology Festival for youth. Many archaeological organizations from all over Washington, DC, and the states of Maryland and Virginia take part. At the festival, there are lots of fascinating exhibits. One year, visitors could see and learn about prehistoric pottery from local sites and then make and decorate pots of their own. There are fun games, too. Children might have to guess what an artifact is and the purpose of that artifact.

66 The trend of all knowledge at the present is to specialize, but archaeology has in it all the qualities that call for the wide view of the human race, of its growth from the savage to the civilized, which is seen in all stages of social and religious development. 99

—Margaret Murray,
Egyptologist and anthropologist

Through these activities, they learn that archaeology is exciting! Alexandra explains, "Archaeology is one of the few fields where you can be the first person to engage with an object or a person that is hundreds or thousands of years old."

Alexandra also runs professional development workshops for college students. They receive mentoring, including help with resumes. They participate in career workshops and meet professionals working in all areas of archaeology.

Alexandra Jones supervising a mock dig

Some students enter into internships with Alexandra. She says, "Internships are a great option for students looking to gain experience in public archaeology." AITC interns gain skills in archaeological programming, education, and fundraising.

The third area of Alexandra's work is her community programs. In 2015, Alexandra began a landscape archaeology project. She paired college students with archaeologists so students could gain a better understanding of the history of Washington, DC.

Students took photographs of archaeological sites in the city and surrounding area in Maryland. The photographs, accompanied by archaeological information, were then displayed and auctioned to raise money for AITC programs.

ARCHAEOLOGY ON TELEVISION

Alexandra's extensive experience running AITC made her the perfect candidate for the Oregon Public Broadcasting series on archaeology, *Time Team America*. In 2012, PBS hired Alexandra to introduce young people to archaeology. She became the program's field school coordinator. Alexandra ran the program's field schools at the Henson House in Maryland, Badger Hole in Oklahoma, Crow Canyon in Colorado, and a Zuni Pueblo in New Mexico.

Lucky participants went on field trips and excavated sites. They tried out scientific illustration and learned how to use archaeological equipment. The young people even learned about stratigraphy by looking at different colors and textures of soil.

Through these experiences, Alexandra increased her students' understanding of archaeology. Students also learned how archaeologists form working relationships with others in their field. It is not possible for one person to be an expert in everything!

Alexandra on *Time Team*

Alexandra's involvement with *Time Team* is different from Chelsea Rose's role, which you read about in the previous chapter. Alexandra organized the Science of Archaeology Field School for kids in middle school and high school who were interested in archaeology. You can read an interview with Alexandra here. How do math, science, and history all relate to each other in the archaeology field?

Time Team Alexandra Jones interview 🔍

Alexandra describes her time with the program as an "awesome experience because I was able to travel nationally and bring together some of the brightest minds in the field to teach my youth all about archaeology."

COMMUNITY ARCHAEOLOGY AROUND THE WORLD

In 2014, Alexandra's work to increase the public's knowledge and understanding of archaeology brought her to the attention of the U.S. State Department.

Gertrude Caton-Thompson

As time passes, soil, rocks, and other types of natural materials settle in strata beneath the earth's surface. The study of these soil layers is called stratigraphy. Unless an area has been disturbed, older artifacts are found in deeper strata and younger artifacts above. A trailblazing British archaeologist named Gertrude Caton-Thompson (1889–1985) used stratigraphy to answer questions about a ruined city called Great Zimbabwe. Colonial white settlers were impressed with the site in Zimbabwe, but they held racist views. They insisted in linking the site to an area mentioned in the Bible because they did not believe that African people could create such great buildings.

The U.S. government had recently signed an agreement with Belize in Central America. The government wanted to help put a stop to the illegal trade of antiquities from Belize's 900 archaeological sites. They were all at risk from looters.

Why is looting a problem? This has been an issue ever since archaeology began. Why do people steal artifacts from archaeological sites and sell them?

photo credit: Royal Anthropological Institute

In 1929, Gertrude proved them wrong. She discovered glass beads, as well as porcelain from China and Persia. Her findings proved that the site was occupied in the 14th century and not during biblical times.

Gertrude received many negative letters from people who were angry about her findings—it was said that she kept these letters in a file labeled "Insane." Why would people write letters like this to her?

The United States could help Belize by funding outreach programs. The goal of these programs was to explain what archaeology is all about and why people should care about it. To help with this understanding, the U.S. State Department invited Alexandra to participate in a series of workshops in Belize.

Alexandra traveled with other experts all around Belize. She was called upon to meet with local business owners and community members.

Dr. Monica Hanna

Dr. Monica Hanna is an Egyptian archaeologist who uses modern-day tools such as Facebook and Twitter. Social media helps her to raise awareness and defend Egypt's cultural heritage from thieves. When she was 14 years old and growing up in Egypt, she snuck into a lab at the Egyptian Museum while on a school trip. She was fascinated, and became a volunteer. This passion grew into a career!

In 2014, she recorded vandals on her cell phone at the Malawi National Museum in Minya, Egypt. They were stealing everything from mummies to scarabs. Thanks to her tweets, people arrived to help her save the remaining artifacts.

They shared ideas. How could Belize's heritage sites be protected? How could they stop the looting? What could be done about the illegal trafficking of Belize's heritage? After all, cultural resources are not renewable. It is not possible to replace a site or an object.

The team brainstormed ideas to encourage something called heritage tourism. This is a type of travel that focuses on the cultural heritage of an area. Heritage tourism can protect the resources of a country.

She received an award for her work from Saving Antiquities for Everyone (SAFE). SAFE works to protect cultural heritage. Monica believes that if archaeological sites are to be protected in Egypt, then young Egyptians must be taught to respect and care for their heritage.

photo credit: Egypt Today

You can learn more about Dr. Hanna and her work at this website.

Egypt Tomb Raiders Monica Hanna 🔍

Ruins in Belize
photo credit: Bernt Rostad

The following year, Alexandra was invited back to Belize to create an interactive archaeology program for young people ages 11 to 15. Her trip was in partnership with the National Institute of Culture and History's Institute of Archaeology in Belize.

Alexandra designed lessons that taught these young people not only about archaeology, but also about why they should preserve their heritage. To ensure that her lessons would engage the students, Alexandra's Belize colleagues added content that was relevant to children in that country.

LOOKING TO THE FUTURE

Thousands of children have discovered archaeology because of Alexandra's dream. Since Alexandra incorporated AITC in 2009, demand for its youth programs has almost doubled. Currently, her programs serve Washington, DC, and the states of Maryland and Virginia. Alexandra reaches many more students around the globe through AITC's website and classroom visits through Skype.

In addition, Alexandra has been able to create opportunities for archaeologists to engage with the public through the planning and organizing of events and through a postcard program. The program had local archaeologists answer questions from children in grades three to five. The responses and the postcards created by local artists were posted online.

Postcard Questions

You can read the postcards from kids at the AITC website. If you were writing a question to an archaeologist, what would you ask? What are you curious about?

Archaeology in Community activities 🔍

As Alexandra looks to the future, she is always thinking of new and creative ways to make archaeology more accessible to people. She creates videos for YouTube, shares photos of artifacts and events on Instagram, and organizes events and connects with communities through Facebook. She also uses a blog to connect with people all over the world.

Alexandra continues to pursue her dreams of reaching more people. She has this advice for girls interested in archaeology.

66 If you love to learn about people and you love science, this is the field for you. You don't have to be the smartest person in the room or the most knowledgeable person, you just have to have a passion for learning and determination not to give up, and you too can be digging up the past. 99

—Alexandra Jones

CHAPTER FOUR
Justine Benanty

Justine Benanty is a maritime archaeologist.
She has investigated slave ships off the coast
of South Africa and participated in digs from
North America to the Middle East. She is
a mentor of Youth Diving with a Purpose,
which engages minorities and at-risk youth
in marine conservation. As the cofounder
of ArchaeoVenturers, she uses new and
innovative technologies to involve the public
in archaeology. She continues to pursue
archaeological studies as a PhD candidate in
underwater cultural heritage management at
the Leiden University in the Netherlands.

Justine grew up in Brooklyn, a neighborhood in New York City, but family vacations allowed Justine to explore places far from the city. She went on family trips to lots of different places, from the American Southwest to Alaska. These trips inspired new interests and hobbies.

Santa Fe, New Mexico, became a special place for Justine. There, she learned to ride horses. Another favorite activity was mountain climbing. She especially loved hiking with her father.

Trilobites

Hiking was something of a treasure hunt, where Justine searched for traces of trees, plants, and marine life preserved in the rocks. Sometimes, Justine came across rare fossils on those dusty trails. These fossils were of prehistoric animals more than 500 million years old! They are trilobites.

At a young age, Justine thought that archaeology and fossil hunting were the same thing. After all, says Justine, they both required a person to dig! It was not until much later that she learned that archaeologists are not fossil hunters. They do not hunt for dinosaur bones.

Professional fossil hunters are called paleontologists. Paleontologists use fossils to tell them more about the history of the earth. Even still, these experiences in Santa Fe contributed to Justine's interest in ancient history.

Each fossil find represented an opportunity to learn more about the past. What happened in the earth's history? How have species changed over time? Justine did not keep her treasures for herself. She donated the fossils to museums, including the Santa Fe Children's Museum, for others to enjoy.

Cool Careers:
Space Archaeologist

Archaeologists use many different types of tools to investigate human culture, including trowels, brushes, laptops, and even satellites. Satellites record variations in the light that is reflected off the surface of the earth. The ground above a buried structure will look different on a satellite image than ground where nothing is buried. Space archaeologists examine images and try to deduce what might be buried there. Then they excavate the site. In 2011, space archaeologist Sarah Parcak discovered potential new sites of ancient pyramids in Egypt.

DREAMING OF ARCHAEOLOGY

In time, Justine forgot about fossils. She found other exciting ways to learn about history. She visited museums. She read lots of books about ancient Egypt. Books also became a way for her to learn about archaeological projects around the world. Justine became captivated by the adventures of a film character named Indiana Jones.

In the movies, Indiana Jones is a bookish archaeology professor who goes on adventures to exotic places, such as Nepal and Egypt. Justine imagined herself going on similar adventures. She was attracted to the series because it mixed history, exploration, and adventure.

When Justine was older, however, she realized that Indiana Jones was a fictional character. While Indiana Jones discovered unknown places, the real world is extensively mapped. But, as the past remains largely unexplored, Justine became determined to investigate it as an archaeologist.

INVESTIGATING ARCHAEOLOGY

Justine's understanding of archaeology was encouraged at her school, Poly Prep Country Day School in Brooklyn, New York. A specialized science course provided her with the opportunity to learn about paleoanthropology.

Paleoanthropologists study ancient footprints, artwork, and tools to learn about our human and pre-human ancestors. Justine's lessons covered fossils and cave paintings. She studied how people used symbols to represent themselves and their world. The course inspired Justine. It connected her interest in the past with a potential career as an archaeologist.

In her junior year, Justine gained more experience for her future career when she was accepted into the High Mountain Institute (HMI) in Leadville, Colorado. The institute is known for its physically demanding and academically challenging programs for teens. At first, Justine found the wilderness experience daunting. Until this point, she had never camped or even put up a tent in her backyard.

HMI expects its students to learn backcountry skills. Justine carried a backpack that weighed about 65 pounds and hiked up to 15 miles a day. Plus, she was expected to hike for weeks in the Rocky Mountains. Justine's determination to try new things drove her to successfully complete a four-day solo trip.

Archaeology in Fiction

The mystery writer Agatha Christie (1890–1976) spent much of her life on digs after marrying archaeologist Max Mallowan. Agatha traveled with him, repairing and cataloging objects. Her experiences in the Middle East

Max Mallowan and Agatha Christie

became part of her novels, such as in *Death on the Nile*. In 1974, archaeologist Barbara Mertz (1927–2013) used her training to write the successful Amelia Peabody mysteries, whose heroine explores Egypt. Today, R.L. LaFevers writes the Theodosia series, which follows the adventures of a smart 11-year-old whose world is filled with mysterious sphinx heads, sacred relics, and "disgruntled dead things." When Theodosia's parents unknowingly bring cursed artifacts into the museum, it is up to her to unravel the hieroglyphics, remove the ancient curse, and outwit a museum thief or two.

> 66 The mountains are calling and I must go. 99

—John Muir,
Scottish-American naturalist

Her confidence continued to build in Colorado when her group reached the summit of Mount Elbert, the state's highest peak. The experience was life-changing. Because of the program, Justine found her passion for the outdoors.

Still in her teens, Justine went on a family trip to the American Museum of Natural History in Alaska. Justine was lucky enough to sit next to the pilot as he landed their plane on a glacier! Justine liked the idea of becoming a pilot. Upon returning to New York, she pursued her pilot's license at a flying school in Long Island. Justine imagines herself one day using her pilot skills to fly crews to remote archaeological sites.

A FOUNDATION FOR THE FUTURE

Justine pursued her childhood dream of becoming an archaeologist at George Washington University (GWU) in Washington, DC. During her first semester, she enrolled in an introduction to archaeology class. It was taught by a well-known biblical archaeologist, Professor Eric Cline. This type of archaeology investigates past cultures and areas mentioned in the Bible.

Two weeks into the class, Justine decided that she would specialize in archaeology. After taking this step, Justine says that she "never looked back." Her professor's encouragement led Justine to go on her first archaeological dig, in Megiddo in northern Israel.

Megiddo was an important city in the ancient world because it was on a major trade route. According to the Bible, Megiddo will be the site of Armageddon, the last battle between good and evil.

Justine joined other volunteers and archaeologists working on the site. It was exciting for her to be in a different country. She had her first chance to work on a site that had some monuments—from temples to palaces—thought to date to the ninth century BCE.

There was so much to be done! Justine began digging before dawn. There were wheelbarrows to push. There were dusty buckets of dirt to haul. It was not a nine-to-five job. Learning the basic skills involved in archaeology could encompass 14 hours a day.

Ask & Answer

Think about what your favorite class at school is. Use details and give two to three reasons about why this class might affect your future goals.

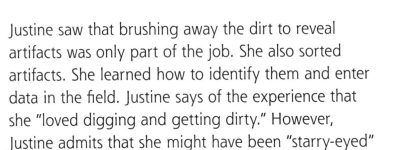

Megiddo

Megiddo has been a very important place for many different cultures since ancient times. It probably gained its importance because of its location. It lies right on the easiest path from northern regions to southern regions of Israel, so traders had to pass through Megiddo. You can learn more about this ancient city at this website.

Archaeology in Community activities 🔍

Justine saw that brushing away the dirt to reveal artifacts was only part of the job. She also sorted artifacts. She learned how to identify them and enter data in the field. Justine says of the experience that she "loved digging and getting dirty." However, Justine admits that she might have been "starry-eyed" at the whole experience.

Justine kept participating in fieldwork while pursuing her undergraduate degree in archaeology, classics, and religion. While pursuing her master's in anthropology with a museum concentration at GWU, she always found time for fieldwork.

One spring, she volunteered at the Shuter's Hill excavation site in Alexandria, Virginia. In the summer of 2010, Justine traveled to Mongolia as an intern. She mapped eleventh-century ruins.

A MARITIME ARCHAEOLOGIST

An event at graduate school changed Justine's life. Maritime archaeologist Dr. Stephen Lubkemann told Justine about an exciting new project called the Slave Wrecks Project (SWP).

SWP was a partnership between several institutions, including Iziko Museums of South Africa, GWU, and the Smithsonian National Museum of African American History and Culture. In 2008, they had formed a partnership to study and preserve artifacts from the transatlantic slave trade.

The professor advised Justine to learn how to scuba dive if she wanted to participate in SWP. Justine had never thought of studying maritime archaeology. She had not known that it was an option.

Justine was inspired in a new direction—the exploration of submerged archaeological sites. She thought maritime archaeology sounded great. As Justine puts it, "Who wouldn't want to dig and dive?"

In 2010, SWP hired Justine as a part-time researcher. She was still in graduate school. Two years later, she was working for them full-time as an associate researcher and project coordinator. Justine took on a variety of roles. She excavated sites in Florida and South Africa. This was her first professional experience as a maritime archaeologist.

As part of her work, Justine sifted through documentation on historic shipwrecks. She scoured the archives of many institutions, including the International Slavery Museum in Liverpool, England. The Iziko Museums of South Africa and South African Heritage Resources Agency in Cape Town, South Africa, were also sources.

Justine's research work was essential to the SWP effort to piece together the complete story of a slave ship called the *São José*. Where was it going? Who was on board? How did it sink? Researchers learned that the ship sank off Cape Town in 1794. Rescuers saved the ship's crew, but only 200 of the more than 500 enslaved Africans from Mozambique.

Transatlantic Slave Trade

From the fifteenth century, traders from Europe began enslaving Africans. Millions of captive people were taken from the African continent by ship to colonies in the Caribbean and to the American mainland. This terrible trade went on for more than 400 years. Many slaves died on the journey. Some ships sank before they reached their destination. The story of these people lay at the bottom of the sea for centuries until marine archaeologists began investigating these wrecks. The people who made it to North America alive were sold into slavery.

In 2014, the SWP began the delicate task of recovering artifacts from the ship. They had remained hidden under the water for nearly 400 years! Recovering artifacts from the ship was not an easy task. The waters off Cape Town are unpredictable.

The sea floor is an unwelcoming environment where the sand and tide constantly rebury objects. Despite these challenges, divers recovered objects from the site. Buried under the sand was a wooden pulley block used to hoist a sail or cargo. They recovered shackles.

Justine says of the experience, "I feel very blessed and privileged and humbled to be a part of a project that gives a voice of those enslaved Africans who, until very recently, have literally been forgotten on the bottom of the sea."

Some of the artifacts that Justine and her fellow archaeologists recovered are part of an exhibit called "Slavery and Freedom." The SWP hopes that artifacts from the *São José* will better educate people about the slave trade.

Ask & Answer

Think about your favorite teacher. How do they encourage you?

The exhibit is part of the new National Museum of African American History and Culture in Washington, DC, that opened in September 2016. Curators with the museum spent more than 10 years collecting artifacts for it.

Conserving Maritime Artifacts

Marine artifacts are fragile. Microorganisms eat away at them as they sit on the sea floor. The sand and the water speed up this deterioration. If these items are left on the sea floor, they will eventually be destroyed. Once marine archaeologists bring these artifacts to the surface, air and light also quickly degrade them. Archaeologists must work quickly to stabilize them.

A wooden object, for example, might crack and split as it dries out. To conserve a wooden object, archaeologists must replace the ocean water with a more stable chemical substance for the object to keep its shape. This process can take weeks or years. You can see a photo of maritime archaeologists working underwater here.

Smithsonian slave wrecks 🔍

To learn more about the history of the *São José*, read an article here.

Smithsonian São José 🔍

According to Justine, "The most challenging part for me is trying to help tell the story of a group of people whose experiences were effectively left out of the written historical texts of their day."

ARCHAEOLOGY AND YOUTH

While working on the *São José* wreck site in Cape Town, Justine discovered her true passion for maritime archaeology. She was fortunate to meet Ken Stewart, who founded the organization Diving With a Purpose (DWP). DWP trains volunteer divers to work with government archaeologists to document and find artifacts in public waters, from lost planes to shipwrecks. Justine and Ken, both native New Yorkers, found that they shared an interest in working with young people.

Because of that interest, Justine and Ken created Youth Diving With a Purpose (YDWP) in 2013. It is a one-of-a-kind program. Diverse and at-risk youth, ages 15 to 23, are given the exciting opportunity to study and help conserve submerged cultural resources.

Justine is the principal archaeologist for the organization. Since the founding of YDWP, Justine has been mentoring kids and working as an instructor with the organization.

Justine works with students from different backgrounds and communities all across the United States. Some students come from as far away as Mozambique in Africa. Over the intense, week-long YDWP experience, Justine trains students to work as a team at Biscayne National Park in Florida. She teaches classes on the land and under the water, where students begin to unravel the secrets of marine archaeology on actual wreck sites.

Justine supervises as students safely investigate ships resting on the sea floor. Students float above wreck sites and practice basic maritime archaeological skills.

Where Are They Now?

YDWP has influenced the careers of many young divers. Some YDWP students have gone on to marine-related studies in college. Justine says of YDWP's students that she is "beyond proud of the young adults that our students have become." She adds, "They are the reason that I keep participating in archaeology and with public education, because it all seems worth it if our next generation is interested in these ideas." You can listen to students speak of their experiences at this website.

YDWP NPS Extraordinary

They use clipboards, pencils, and tape measures to document and map the debris field of a wreck and draw artifacts as they are found. YDWP has also teamed up with the Coral Restoration Foundation, based in the Florida Keys. Students are now planting and restoring coral reefs.

In the summer of 2016, Justine traveled to Mozambique, where YDWP students participated in dives to slave wrecks for the first time. Justine's conversation with Ken all those years ago has resulted in many young people participating in marine conservation and archaeology.

YDWP has grown into a federally recognized program. In 2014, it was designated a Preserve America Steward by former First Lady Michelle Obama.

ADVENTURES IN ARCHAEOLOGY

Digital technology has helped Justine increase the public's understanding of what archaeology is all about. In 2014, she launched ArchaeoVenturers. Her co-creator was fellow GWU alumna Katie Paul.

Through its web presence, the company has become a resource for young archaeologists. Justine also saw students using it as an outlet to increase the visibility of their work before the public.

Coral reefs

To engage the next generation of archaeologists, Justine is creating original YouTube content and incorporating other social technologies with ArchaeoVenturers. Her hope is that young people will use the company's site to connect with archaeological resources and to find role models.

The idea of showcasing role models is important. Justine did not discover a female STEM figure that she could relate to until high school. STEM stands for science, technology, engineering and math. In high school, Justine read a book by primatologist and conservationist Mireya Mayor. Justine related to Mireya because, like herself, Mireya "could get dirty in the field but wear pink boots and be totally confident with herself personally and professionally."

LOOKING TO THE FUTURE

A love for digging in the dirt is important for many branches of archaeology. But for marine archaeology, you need to have a love for scuba diving and the ocean. "If you can't swim," says Justine, "how can you know the ocean depths?" And if you don't know the ocean depths, then you won't be able to find shipwrecks, ancient sunken cities, and other objects that tell stories of long ago.

Justine believes that archaeologists need to be adaptable and eager to learn new skills. They never know where their next fieldwork opportunity might take them. Living and working conditions vary from country to country. "Perhaps most importantly," says Justine, "you need to have a lot of patience and love the pursuit of knowledge."

66 I want to set the example my mother set for me: a strong female role model who faces challenges, takes risks, and conquers fears. I want my children to know that as women, they can do whatever they dream as long as they believe in themselves. More than anything, it is my responsibility to instill in my daughters the knowledge that they can have a family and everything else too. 99

—Mireya Mayor,
scientist, explorer, wildlife correspondent, and anthropologist

Justine has created an exciting career by surrounding herself with supportive people. "Believe that only the sky is the limit," says Justine, adding "Maybe not even that—why not shoot for the stars?"

Justine advises girls to aim high. She has seen many girls succeed in marine biology or marine engineering. Justine says that she "wants to live in a world where [girls in STEM] are the norm, not the exception, and I hope that I am able to help drive even a small part of that change through these various projects."

#FieldworkFace

Wanting to showcase who archaeologists are and what they do led Justine to create a hashtag for the social media sites Twitter and Facebook. Her hashtag was Show off YOUR #FieldworkFace. Archaeologists uploaded photos of themselves with the hashtag so that the public would see actual archaeologists in the field. Archaeologists' selfies revealed them digging trenches, hiking through woods, taking notes on a laptop while sitting in front of a 4,000-year-old rock painting, and much more. To see photographs from the project visit this website.

Twitter, #FieldworkFace 🔍

Sixth Century BCE

- Ennigaldi curates the first museum in the ancient city of Ur.

Fifteenth Century

- Isabella d'Este Gonzaga (1474–1539) becomes an important patron of poets, writers, and artists.

Nineteenth Century

- Charlotte Schreiber (1812–1895) builds one of the finest collections of china in the world.
- Caroline Bonaparte Murat (1782–1839) takes an interest in preserving the ruins of Pompeii.

1873

- Amelia Edwards (1831–1892) devotes her life to raising money for the study and protection of Egyptian archaeological sites after traveling to Egypt.

1881

- Jane Dieulafoy (1851–1916) gives lectures, publishes her writing, and organizes an exhibition of antiquities at the Louvre Museum after excavations in the ancient city of Susa.

1900

- Harriet Boyd Hawes (1871–1945) arrives on the island of Crete and during the next few years excavates the Bronze Age town of Gournia.

1924

- Gertrude Bell (1868–1926) writes the first laws to protect Iraq's artifacts from being looted. Two years later, she founds the Baghdad Archaeological Museum.

1929

- Gertrude Caton-Thompson (1889–1985) uses stratigraphy to establish the date of the city of Great Zimbabwe.

1929

- Bertha Parker Pallan (1907–1978), one of the first Native American archeologists, excavates a pueblo site in Nevada.

1930

- Agatha Christie (1890–1976) works on sites and incorporates archaeological themes into some of her crime novels.

1948

- Mary Douglas Leakey (1913–1996) makes her first of many discoveries in Africa when she finds fragments of a skull of an ape that lived 14 to 23 million years ago.

1960s

- Wilhelmina Jashemski (1910–2007) establishes the field of garden archaeology.

1975

- Barbara Mertz (1927–2013) publishes the first Amelia Peabody novel using her experience and training as an Egyptologist.

1993

- Kathleen Deagan (1948–) finds evidence of the 16th-century campsite of Pedro Menendez de Aviles.

1998

- Constanza Ceruti (1973–) is part of a team of researchers who discover 500-year-old Inca bodies on Mount Llullaillaco, Argentina.

2000

- Mireya Mayor (1973–) co-discovers the smallest primate in the world, the Microcebus, or mouse lemur.

2006

- Alexandra Jones founds Archaeology in the Community.

2010

- Justine Benanty begins her work with the Slave Wrecks Project.

2013

- Dr. Monica Hanna uses Twitter to stop looters from stealing antiquities from Malawi National Museum in Egypt.

2014

- Kristina Killgrove (1977–) begins her studies of the skeletons of ancient Romans.

2015

- Sarah Parcak (1979–), on the southwestern coast of Newfoundland, locates what may be North America's second Viking settlement.

Introduction

- What is archaeology? How do archaeologists use artifacts to deepen our knowledge of past people and cultures?

Chapter 1

- Have you ever collected stamps, coins, or rocks? What did you learn from your collection? If you were to start a new collection, what would it be and why? How would you share this collection with family and friends?

- Today, modern archaeologists often do not excavate an entire site but investigate only a portion of it. Imagine that you have been asked to investigate a historical site near you, which has written records. How would records, including diaries and newspapers, help you in your investigation?

- Using a Venn diagram, compare and contrast drawing and photography. Think about reasons why archaeologists record their findings and how they could use these images.

- Why is it important for women to have the same career opportunities as men?

- Archaeologists conduct research before, during, and after a dig. A report done by the Canadian government suggested that archaeologists spend 10 minutes doing paperwork for every minute they dig. What do you think are the benefits of record keeping during and after a dig? How would a person use these records in the future?

Chapter 2

- Write down three things you were interested when you were younger. Next, write down three things you are interested in now. Compare the lists. What do you notice? How have your interests changed and how have they stayed the same?

- Why is it important to study different cultures from different points of view?

- What does teamwork mean to you? Give an example of a time when you worked on a project with several other people. What was it like?

Chapter 3

- Why do you think that it is important to set goals? On a piece of paper, write down one of your goals. Next, write down three simple steps to take to help you achieve this goal.

- Think about a field trip that you enjoyed and the hands-on activities that you participated in. How did these activities change your knowledge of the subject that you were studying? Why are hands-on activities useful when learning about a topic?

- Why do you think it is important to follow your dreams? Who in your life has encouraged you to dream bigger?

- Is there something you want to be learning while you're a kid that is missing from your education? How can you make that learning happen?

- Why do you think it is important to preserve historic sites? With an adult's permission, investigate a site near you to find out how it is being protected and preserved.

Chapter 4

- If you could create a new archaeological series where would your heroine travel? What type of archaeology would she be involved in and why?

- Think about what your favorite class at school is. Use details and give two to three reasons about why this class might affect your future goals.

- Who is your favorite teacher? How do they encourage you?

abroad: out of one's own country.

analyze: to make a careful study.

ancestor: someone from your family or culture who lived before you.

anthology: a collection of poems by different authors.

anthropology: the study of human culture and human development.

antiquities: objects from ancient times.

archaeologist: a scientist who studies ancient people and their cultures by finding and examining things such as graves, ruins, tools, and pottery.

architecture: the style or look of a building.

archivist: a person who cares for an extensive record or collection of papers.

artifact: any man-made object that archaeologists study to learn about an ancient civilization.

BCE: put after a date, BCE stands for Before Common Era and counts down to zero. CE stands for Common Era and counts up from zero. These nonreligious terms correspond to BC and AD. This book was printed in 2017 CE.

bias: a way of looking at or thinking about something that might be wrong or unfair or limiting.

bioarchaeologist: an archaeologist who studies human remains found in archaeological sites.

biological anthropology: the study of how people have evolved and adapted to their environment.

biology: the study of life and of living things.

blog: a regularly updated website or web page, by an individual or small group, that is written in an informal or conversational style. Short for weblog.

bog iron: a type of iron found in bogs or swamps.

Bronze Age: the period of human culture characterized by the use of bronze tools, beginning about or before 3500 BCE.

capital: the topmost part of a column.

career: a person's occupation, with opportunities for progress.

cataloguing: organizing and classifying.

Celtic: Irish and Scottish.

census: an official count or survey of a population that records various details about individuals.

civilization: a community of people that is advanced in art, science, and government.

classical archaeologist: an archaeologist whose work focuses on ancient peoples such as the Egyptian and Roman civilizations.

classical languages: Greek and Latin.

Glossary

classify: to put things in groups based on what they have in common.

collaborate: to work with others.

colony: a country or area that is under the part or full political control of another country.

commission: an instruction given to another person, such as an artist, for a piece of work.

community archaeology: archaeology that is started and done by a local community.

conservation: managing and protecting something, such as natural resources or an archaeological site.

context: the surrounding area in which an artifact is found.

coral reef: an underwater ecosystem that grows in warm ocean waters and is home to millions of creatures.

cultural anthropology: the study of culture, including language, law, politics, and art.

culture: a group of people who share beliefs and a way of life.

curate: to care for a collection of something.

customs: traditions or ways of doing things, including dress, food, and holidays.

descendent: a person related to someone who lived in the past.

document: to make a written record of something.

drought: a long period of dry weather, especially one that damages crops.

Egyptologist: someone who studies Egypt.

enamel: to coat a piece of art with a glassy substance for decoration and protection.

environment: everything in nature, living and nonliving, including plants, animals, soil, rocks, and water.

erupt: to burst out suddenly, such as in a volcano.

excavate: to dig out a site and its artifacts for study.

fiction: stories that describe imaginary events and people.

field: a place to do research out in the natural world rather than in a laboratory.

fieldwork: collecting information at an actual site rather than in a lab.

fossil: the remains of any organism, including animals and plants, that have been preserved in rock.

fresco: a work of art painted with pigment on wet plaster on a wall or ceiling.

galleon: a sailing ship used before the eighteenth century.

garden archaeologist: an archaeologist who excavates and restores ancient gardens.

geography: the study of the earth and its features, especially the shape of the land, and the effect of human activity.

Gold Rush: the period of time in American history during the 1800s when people rushed to the West in search of gold.

grid: a series of evenly spaced horizontal and vertical lines.

hearth: an open fireplace.

heritage: the art, buildings, traditions, and beliefs that are important to a country's or the world's history.

hieroglyphics: a type of writing system that uses pictures and symbols called hieroglyphs (or just glyphs) to represent words and ideas.

historian: an expert in history, especially of a particular period of time or geographical region.

historical archaeologist: an archaeologist whose work focuses on cultures of the modern world.

homesteader: a person who settled and farmed land during the 1800s, especially under the Homestead Act.

humanity: all people.

image: a picture of something, either real or imagined.

indigenous: native to a place.

internship: a training period in service of an employer.

interpret: to think about something and explain it.

Iron Age: the period of human culture characterized by the smelting of iron and its use in industry, beginning around 1000 BCE.

landscape: a large area of land with specific features.

lava: hot, melted rock that has risen to the surface of the earth.

linguistic: having to do with the study of languages.

maritime archaeologist: an archaeologist whose work focuses on human interaction with the ocean and other bodies of water.

master's degree: an advanced degree from a college or university that represents mastery in a specific field of study.

medallion: a piece of jewelry in the shape of a medal.

media: the industry in the business of presenting news to the public by methods including radio, television, Internet, and newspapers.

medieval: describes the Middle Ages, the period of European history after the fall of the Roman Empire, from about 350 to 1450 CE.

medium: the material artists use to create their art, such as stone, paint, and ink.

mentor: a person who advises and guides a younger person.

merchant: a person who buys and sells goods for a profit.

Mesopotamia: an area of ancient civilization between the Tigris and Euphrates Rivers in what is now called Iraq, Kuwait, and Syria.

microorganism: a living organism that is so small you can only see it with a microscope.

Middle Ages: the period of European history after the fall of the Roman Empire, from about 350 to 1450 CE.

Glossary

middle class: the section of society between the poor and the wealthy, including business and professional people and skilled workers.

minaret: a slender tower.

mining claim: the legal control of an area where minerals, such as gold, are found in the ground.

minority: a group of people, such as African Americans, that is smaller than or different from the larger group. Also less than half of the people or voters.

mock dig: an archaeological site that is created for the purpose of teaching about archaeology.

monument: a building, structure, or statue that is special because it honors an event or person, or because it is beautiful.

myth: a traditional story that expresses the beliefs and values of a group of people.

nobility: in the past, the people considered to be the most important in a society.

nonprofit: an organization supported by donations whose main mission is to help people, animals, the environment, or other causes.

paleoanthropologist: a scientist who studies the fossilized remains of prehistoric humans.

paleoethnobotany: the study of the remains of plants grown or used by people in ancient times, which have survived in archaeological sites.

Paleolithic: the first part of the Stone Age, which lasted until about 12,000 years ago.

paleontologist: a scientist who studies fossils.

patron: a person who gives financial support to a person or organization.

peer: a person in your group.

petroglyph: a rock carving.

pharaoh: the title for ancient Egyptian kings or rulers.

PhD: stands for Doctor of Philosophy. A PhD is the highest degree in an area of study given by a college or university.

pictograph: a rock painting.

pioneer: one of the first to use or apply a new area of knowledge, or one of the first to settle in a new land.

porcelain: a type of white pottery that is thin, smooth, and shiny.

prehistoric archaeologist: an archaeologist who investigates the world as it was before there was writing.

prehistoric: long ago, before written history.

Preserve America Stewards: a designation for a program that uses volunteers to care for historical sites.

preservation: taking care of something, preserving it.

primatologist: a scientist who studies primates. These are mammals that have large brains, nails on the hands and feet, and a short snout. Apes, monkeys, chimpanzees, and humans are primates.

professional development: training and education for people working in specific careers.

racist: hatred of people of a different race.

radar: a device that detects objects by bouncing radio waves off them and measuring how long it takes for the waves to return.

Renaissance: a period of time in Europe after the Middle Ages, from the 1300s to the 1600s.

research: the planned investigation and study of something to discover facts and reach conclusions.

resume: a formal statement of your education and experience.

role model: someone who inspires others.

ruin: a building or area that has fallen into disrepair.

satellite: a device that orbits the earth to relay communication signals or transmit information.

scarabs: carved beetles that were popular in ancient Egypt.

sculpture: carved stone, wood, or other material.

settlement: a place where a group of people moves to start a new community.

site: the position of something in connection with its surroundings.

smelt: to extract metal from rock by heating and melting.

space archaeologist: an archaeologist who uses satellites to find sites for excavation.

species: a group of plants or animals that are closely related and produce offspring.

stereotype: to make a judgment about a group of individuals. The inaccurate belief that all people who share a single physical or cultural trait are the same.

strata: layers.

stratigraphy: the study of the layers of material that are found in archaeological excavation.

survey: to examine or measure something.

technology: the tools, methods, and systems used to solve a problem or do work.

thesis: an important paper written by a student as part of their college degree.

tourism: the business of people traveling for pleasure.

trilobite: an extinct marine animal.

tripod: a three-legged support.

trowel: a small, hand-held shovel.

turf: the grass and the layer of earth held by the grass roots.

urbanization: becoming more like a city.

Venn diagram: a diagram that uses circles to represent sets and their relationships.

Vikings: a group of seafaring pirates and traders from Scandinavia who migrated throughout Europe between the eighth and eleventh centuries.

virtual media: a way of connecting a remote media source to a local system.

zooarchaeology: the study of the remains of animals, such as bones, shells, and scales.

Resources

Books

- Capek, Michael. *Unsolved Archaeological Mysteries.* North Mankato, Minnesota: Capstone, 2015.

- Macdonald, Fiona. *Amazing Archaeologists: True Stories of Astounding Archaeological Discoveries.* Chicago: Raintree, 2014.

- Steele, Kathryn. *Stones and Bones: Archaeology in Action.* New York: PowerKids, 2013.

- White, John R. *Hands-on Archaeology: Real-life Activities for Kids.* Waco, Texas: Prufrock, 2005.

Websites

- Archaeology for Kids:
  archaeology.mrdonn.org

- British Museum: Ancient Egypt:
  ancientegypt.co.uk/menu.html

- Colonial Williamsburg: Games/Activities:
  history.org/kids/games/dirtDetective.cfm

- National Park Service: Archaeology for Kids:
  nps.gov/archeology/public/kids/index.htm

- Reed Farmstead Kids Archaeological Site:
  kidsdigreed.com

- Museum of Underwater Archaeology:
  mua.apps.uri.edu/HTMLTEST/childrens.htm

- Written in Bone:
  anthropology.si.edu/writteninbone

Resources

QR Code Glossary

- Page 9: penn.museum/sites/iraq
- Page 10: getty.edu/education/teachers/ classroom_resources/tips_tools/cabinet.html
- Page 19: griffith.ox.ac.uk/edwards-special
- Page 23: chnm.gmu.edu/ worldhistorysources/r/57/whm.html
- Page 25: appliedcomicsetc.com/portfolio/gertrude
- Page 26: gournia.org
- Page 36: nps.gov/labe/learn/historyculture/rockart.htm
- Page 45: mailtribune.com/article/20090428/ NEWS/904280325
- Page 51: romandnaproject.org
- Page 52: youtube.com/watch?v = yqD-csTWorI
- Page 57: pbslearningmedia.org/resource/12c75c61- d8bd-4be9-8aac-06598bab68f4/12c75c61- d8bd-4be9-8aac-06598bab68f4
- Page 67: pbs.org/time-team/field-school/engage-youth-stem
- Page 71: youtube.com/watch?v = THQ6HacY3oc
- Page 73: archaeologyincommunity.com/activities-section
- Page 83: sites.google.com/site/megiddoexpedition
- Page 87: newsdesk.si.edu/photos/slave-wrecks- project-s-o-jos-underwater-archaeology-image-1
- Page 87: newsdesk.si.edu/factsheets/ history-s-o-jos-slave-ship-and-site
- Page 89: youtube.com/watch?v = SOoTre8XgrM
- Page 93: imgrum.net/tag/fieldworkface

Index

Index

Index